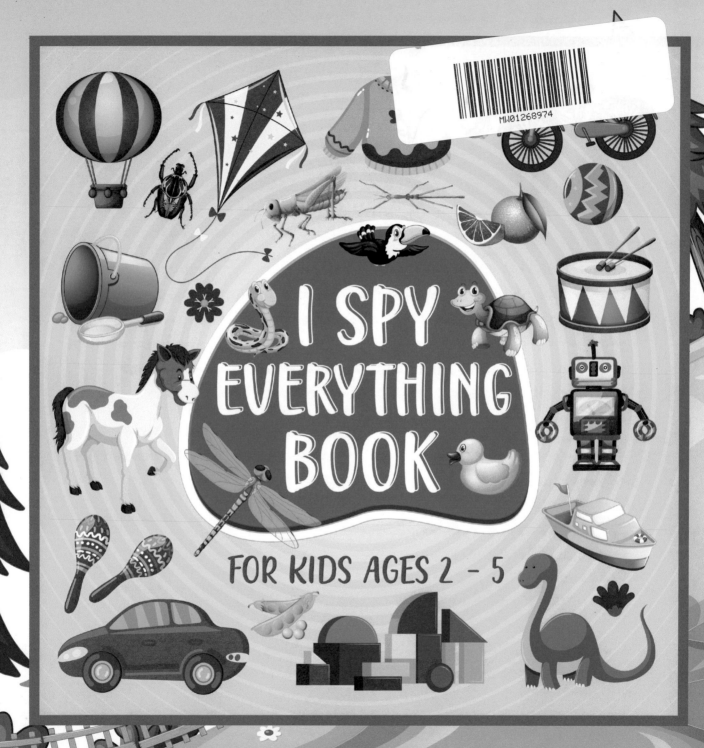

I SPY EVERYTHING BOOK

FOR KIDS AGES 2 - 5

This Book Belongs To

_____

_____

_____

This book is especially
designed for the Animal
lover toddlers and
preschoolers.
It will increase their visual
ability, problem solving skills
and concentration.

Best Wishes!

- Childful Publishing

I SPY with my little eye something beginning with...

A AND B

A is for Aeroplane

B is for Ball

I SPY with my little eye something beginning with...

C AND D

C
is for
Car

D
is for
Drum

I SPY with my little eye something beginning with...

E AND F

E is for

Elephant

F is for

Fish

I SPY with my little eye something beginning with...

G AND H

G is for

Grapes

H is for

Hat

I SPY with my little eye something beginning with...

AND

I is for

Ice-Cream

J is for

Juice

I SPY with my little eye something beginning with...

K AND L

K is for Knife

L is for Lobster

I SPY with my little eye something beginning with...

M AND N

M is for Mango

N is for Nest

I SPY with my little eye something beginning with...

O AND P

O is for

Owl

P is for

Pineapple

I SPY with my little eye something beginning with...

Q AND R

Q is for Quiver

R is for Rabbit

I SPY with my little eye something beginning with...

S  AND T

S is for Snake

T is for Tree

I SPY with my little eye something beginning with...

U AND V

U is for

Umbrella

V is for

Vase

I SPY with my little eye something beginning with...

W AND X

W is for

Watermelon

X is for

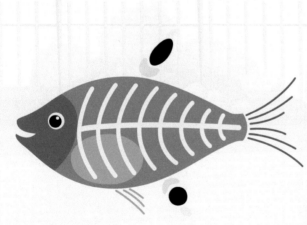

X-ray Fish

I SPY with my little eye something beginning with...

Y AND Z

Y is for

Yacht

Z is for

Zebra

I Spy 3 Missing Things

I Spied 3 Missing Things

I Spy Things in Red

I Spied Things in Red

I Spy Things in Blue

I Spied Things in Blue

I Spy Things in Green

I Spied Things in Green

I Spy Things in Yellow

I Spied Things in Yellow

16361767R00026